PIANO • VOCAL • GUITAR

Pinocchio

All songs in this publication are the property of:

Bourne Co.
Music Publishers
www.bournemusic.com

ISBN 978-1-5400-5300-8

BOURNE CO.
New York

DISTRIBUTED BY

Visit Hal Leonard Online at
www.halleonard.com

Contact us:
Hal Leonard
7777 West Bluemound Road
Milwaukee, WI 53213
Email: info@halleonard.com

In Europe, contact:
Hal Leonard Europe Limited
42 Wigmore Street
Marylebone, London, W1U 2RN
Email: info@halleonardeurope.com

In Australia, contact:
Hal Leonard Australia Pty. Ltd.
4 Lentara Court
Cheltenham, Victoria, 3192 Australia
Email: info@halleonard.com.au

GIVE A LITTLE WHISTLE

Words by NED WASHINGTON
Music by LEIGH HARLINE

HI-DIDDLE-DEE-DEE
(An Actor's Life for Me)

Words by NED WASHINGTON
Music by LEIGH HARLINE

HONEST JOHN

Words by NED WASHINGTON
Music by LEIGH HARLINE

I'VE GOT NO STRINGS

Words by NED WASHINGTON
Music by LEIGH HARLINE

Why does the gay lit-tle dick-y bird sing? What put the zing in a but-ter-fly's wing?

What's the rea-son for the smile of a trou-ba-dour?

Why does a breeze have a bar-rel of fun? E-ven the bee who's a

LITTLE WOODEN HEAD

Words by NED WASHINGTON
Music by LEIGH HARLINE

JIMINY CRICKET

Words by NED WASHINGTON
Music by LEIGH HARLINE

MONSTRO THE WHALE

Words by NED WASHINGTON
Music by LEIGH HARLINE

THREE CHEERS FOR ANYTHING

Words by NED WASHINGTON
Music by LEIGH HARLINE

TURN ON THE OLD MUSIC BOX

Words by NED WASHINGTON
Music by LEIGH HARLINE

WHEN YOU WISH UPON A STAR

Words by NED WASHINGTON
Music by LEIGH HARLINE